D1603881

THE Golden Carot

THE VISCONTI-SFORZA DECK

MARY PACKARD

CARD ILLUSTRATIONS BY RACHEL CLOWES

FOREWORD BY ROBERT M. PLACE

Race Point
PUBLISHING
www.QuartoKnows.com
New York, NY

Brimming with creative inspiration, how-to projects, and useful
information to enrich your everyday life, Quarto Knows is a favorite
destination for those pursuing their interests and passions. Visit our
site and dig deeper with our books into your area of interest:
Quarto Creates, Quarto Cooks, Quarto Homes, Quarto Lives,
Quarto Drives, Quarto Explores, Quarto Gifts, or Quarto Kids.

First published in 2013 by Race Point Publishing, an imprint of The Quarto Group,
142 West 36th Street 4th Floor, New York, NY 10018, USA
T (212) 779-4972 **F** (212) 779-6058 **www.QuartoKnows.com**

This 2013 edition published by Race Point Publishing by arrangement with
The Book Shop, Ltd.

Race Point Publishing titles are also available at discount for retail, wholesale,
promotional, and bulk purchase. For details, contact the Special Sales Manager by
email at specialsales@quarto.com or by mail at The Quarto Group, Attn: Special Sales
Manager, 100 Cummings Center, Suite 265D, Beverly, MA 01915, USA.

DESIGN: Tim Palin Creative

ISBN-13: 978-1-937994-09-9

Printed in China

6 8 10 9 7

CONTENTS

FOREWORD

Decks of playing cards have existed in Europe since the fourteenth century. The earliest deck was composed of four suits and was structured like a modern deck with ten pips and three courts in each suit, except the suits were coins, cups, swords, and batons. In Renaissance Italy, between 1410 and 1442, four queens and a fifth suit, composed of a parade of mystical enigmatic figures, were added to this deck, and the Tarot was born.

Since the late eighteenth century, occultists have considered the Tarot an indispensable part of their magical equipment. To provide it with what they considered to be a suitable ancient pedigree, they made up numerous spurious histories and associations for the deck. It was given an origin in ancient Egypt and said to be the creation of ancient Kabalists or of Egyptian priests under the guidance of the mythical sage Hermes Trismegistus. Not all of the insights of the occultists were wrong, but these assertions are false. At their worst, the occultists' associations have become a wall of confusion that blocks one from appreciating the mystical heritage that is preserved in the deck.

The closest we can come to an appreciation of the Tarot's authentic tradition is to contemplate the oldest existing cards. All of the early examples are sumptuous miniature works of art composed of paint and gold leaf on heavy paper and designed by artists for noble patrons. All of these decks are missing cards. Fifteen of the existing decks were created for the Visconti family, the rulers of Milan. One of those decks, the Visconti-Sforza Tarot, has the distinction of being the most complete of all of the earliest decks. Here we can see for the first time a deck with a Fool and nineteen of the twenty-one trumps that are now considered standard (only the Devil and the Tower are absent). In fact, in 1499, when Milan was conquered by Louis XII of France, the Tarot of Milan became the model for the French deck, known as the Tarot of Marseilles, which was later discovered by the occultists and came to be considered the standard for the world.

In *The Golden Tarot*, Mary Packard does an excellent job of reintroducing the Visconti-Sforza Tarot to a modern audience. She provides insights into its history and symbolism and has an appreciation for its beauty and for its usefulness in divination. Once again, we can see that the Tarot expresses a timeless mystical philosophy, which is an inheritance that we cannot afford to lose.

Robert M. Place

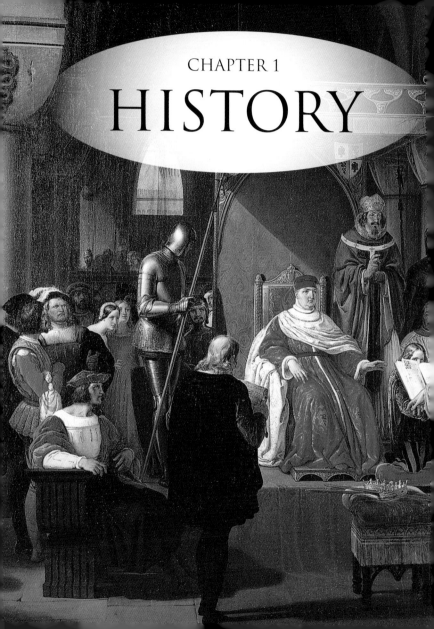

CHAPTER 1
HISTORY

How would a rich and powerful nobleman living in Milan in the mid-1400s commemorate a birth, a wedding, or an anniversary? A portrait would be a fine choice were it not so yesterday. A gala would be great fun, but over so quickly. No, it would have to be something both lasting and unique—an undertaking available only to those with illustrious social connections and substantial wealth. The new trend of commissioning a deck of playing cards would fit the bill to a tee. Painted by gifted artists, the cards were an original way for an aristocrat to mark a momentous occasion and showcase his exalted station.

Often, the painted cards featured members of the commissioning family dressed in their finest garments and posed in elaborate settings. These cards offered future generations a fascinating if idealized glimpse into the lives of the nobility who flourished in that time and place. One of the oldest and most complete surviving decks of playing cards was commissioned by Milan's ruling family, the Visconti-Sforzas.

Previous page: *Filippo Maria Visconti, the Duke of Milan, is shown restoring the crown to the kings of Aragon and Navarra in this nineteenth-century painting by Francesco Hayez.*

FAMILY TIES

Duke Filippo Maria Visconti was said to have been the richest man in Italy, but even for him, life was not problem free. Because fifteenth-century Italy consisted of so many warring city states, it was anything but peaceful. The duke, like other landed gentry, was in a state of constant alert against the possibility of an army of marauding invaders showing up to threaten his holdings.

And then there was the matter of Visconti's infertility. Although he was married several times, he was unable to produce heirs—specifically, a son to inherit his title. When he was finally presented with a daughter in 1425, he was overjoyed. The fact that she was female and born out of wedlock did nothing to dampen his delight. He named her Bianca Maria. Visconti doted on his only child and provided her with a first-class education that included schooling in the Latin classics, music, art, science, and math. Both father and daughter shared a love for hunting and for horses.

SOLDIERS OF FORTUNE

The Sforza family interests lay elsewhere. Muzio Attendolo, founder of the Sforza dynasty, was descended from a prosperous farming family. But the rural life was not for him. He left home at a young age to train with the condotierri, soldiers hired to defend a duchy or kingdom against invaders. Attendolo's formidable military skills won him the name of *Sforza*, which means "strong" in Italian. The name stuck, and it wasn't long before he formed his own army of mercenaries. His son Francesco assumed control after Muzio drowned in 1424. Under Francesco's command, the army became the most powerful in Italy.

When Filippo Visconti found himself under attack, he called upon Francesco Sforza to lead an army against the invading Venetians. It was the custom at the time to expand and solidify the power of the nobility through marriage. And so it was that Visconti pledged Bianca Maria's hand to Sforza as a reward for his military success. The wedding took place on October 25, 1441.

Opposite page: *The wedding of Francesco Sforza and Bianca Maria Visconti*

ANNIVERSARY CARDS

Due to the complications of succession, the dukedom of Milan did not automatically fall to Francesco Sforza when Visconti died. Sforza was forced to win his father-in-law's title through battle. The opposing forces were no match for Sforza, and Milan surrendered to him in 1450.

The Visconti-Sforza marriage proved to be a successful one with many heirs. Bianca Maria involved herself in all the affairs of state, becoming active as a patron of hospitals, churches, and the arts. In 1448, her popularity grew to legendary proportions when she donned a suit of armor and joined in battle against another onslaught of Venetian invaders. It was this episode that earned her the nickname Warrior Woman.

On the occasion of their tenth wedding anniversary in 1451, Francesco Sforza hired the well-known artist Bonifacio Bembo to create a deck of cards in their honor. The couple, wearing costumes typical of the first half of the fifteenth century, is featured individually and together on some of the cards. It's poignant to note the disparity between the seemingly refined and fragile maiden depicted on the cards with Bianca Maria's legendary Warrior Woman persona. The contrast speaks eloquently of a desire for more peaceful moments—free from the threat of plundering armies.

ITALIAN PAGEANTRY

One of the important traditions that influenced the creation of the Visconti-Sforza cards was the popularity of triumphs. Originally held in ancient Rome, triumphs were parades created for the purpose of celebrating victorious generals. Each contingent of a Roman triumph was followed by a group who trumped them in importance. Prisoners, the lowest of the participants, led the parade. Directly behind them marched their captors, who were followed by their superiors, and so on, until at the very end, the conquering general appeared amidst great fanfare.

Centuries later, the Roman triumphs lost their military focus and were replaced with parades resplendent with religious pageantry. During the Middle Ages, it was not unusual to see one of these processions—a donkey cart laden with religious artifacts followed by clergy—wending its way through the narrow Tuscan streets. The clergy, dressed in luxurious robes, would have strolled solemnly to the strains of liturgical music played by musicians who were also splendidly clad.

The figures portrayed on the Lovers card are thought to be Francesco Sforza and Bianca Maria Visconti.

By the dawn of the Renaissance, so named because it was a time of renewed interest in all things classical, the elaborate religious processions had merged with festive secular parades to re-create a stepped-up version of the Roman triumph. Gleaming horse-drawn chariots filled with well-known heroic and villainous figures were accompanied by singers, dancers, and colorfully clad performance artists.

Similar in nature to a modern-day Mardi Gras pageant, the triumphs were enacted on a variety of occasions, such as weddings, funerals, and important holidays. Major artists of the day were called upon to direct the pageants and design sumptuous costumes and glittering scenery for the floats. Many of these stylistic elements are reflected in the costumes and scenery depicted on the Visconti-Sforza Tarot cards.

Sometimes, Renaissance triumphs featured performers who embodied Plato's virtues. Uniting the basic hierarchical form of the triumph with themes that were complex and allegorical in nature, these pageants presented a procession of virtues, each trumping the other in importance.

Classical themes were revived in Renaissance art and literature as well. Paintings depicting Plato's four cardinal virtues—Prudence, Justice, Fortitude, and Temperance— were popular subjects for artists. Similarly, for writers and poets of the day, the theme of the virtues superseding each other and finally trumping Evil was an ever popular topic. Characters from Dante's *Divine Comedy*, and Petrarch's six-part poem *I Trionfi* would have been familiar to everyone, even commoners.

In *I Trionfi*, Petarch describes a young man who returns to the place where he met his first love, a beautiful young maiden named Laura. He falls asleep under a tree and dreams of life as a triumph. When man is young, he is conquered by Love. As he grows older, Chastity vanquishes Love. Death triumphs over Chastity, but Fame beats Death by allowing man's name to live on. Eventually, however, Fame loses out to Time. Only Eternity, in the form of eternal life, can conquer Time.

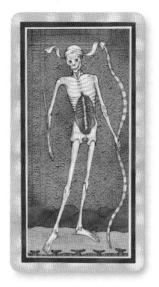

It is not at all surprising that some of the images and themes made familiar by the painters and writers of the day would appear on Visconti-Sforza cards, since both the card game and the arts emerged from the same cultural tradition.

The Death card from the Visconti-Sforza deck

THE GAME

Although it is likely that cards had been used for divination by this time, the purpose of the Visconti-Sforza cards was to play a game called Triumphs. The ancestor of Bridge, the game took its name directly from the Renaissance parades. In Italian, the game is called *Trionfi*, from which the English word *trump* is derived.

The deck used to play a game of Triumphs is made up of seventy-eight cards. Fifty-six cards are evenly divided among four suits—swords, coins, batons, and cups. The fifth suit consists of twenty-one picture cards plus a Fool that functions as a wild card. It is the fifth suit, the trumps, that distinguishes these newly invented cards, called Tarot, from all others.

Images depicted on the Visconti-Sforza trump cards are of standardized Renaissance subjects—for example, the Sun, the Moon, and the virtues of Fortitude and Temperance. The illustrations on the trumps of other Tarot decks vary, depending on the artist and on the time and place that the cards were created. However, despite the differences in the pictures, slight variations in the names of the trumps, and an altered sequence here and there, Tarot decks are more similar to each other than not.

The Visconti-Sforza trump cards differ from other Tarot cards in that they are not numbered. But although they lack numbers, they are still sequential in value, with the lowest trump card in the deck being the Magician, and the highest trump, the World.

Opposite page: *Two people participate in a game of Tarot in this detail of a sixteenth-century fresco by Niccolò dell'Abate.*

ELEMENTS OF STYLE

Artist Bonifacio Bembo's extensive experience painting miniatures for illuminated manuscripts made him an excellent choice to create the art for most of the cards. Each exquisite hand-painted card in the Visconti-Sforza deck is a tiny masterpiece. The scenes are lavishly executed in gold leaf and paints made with powdered lapis lazuli, malachite, and other precious minerals. The predominant colors are gold, red, and blue, and intricate patterns decorate the backgrounds and much of the clothing.

In composition, the cards are reminiscent of the style perfected by Leonardo da Vinci, whom records show was called upon to direct at least two triumphs. Leonardo's influence can be seen in the sense of depth created by the breaking away of the ground at the bottom front of several of the Visconti-Sforza cards, including the Moon (right), Star, Sun, Death, and Temperance.

THE FIRST TAROT DECKS

The Visconti-Sforza deck is the most complete of the fifteen oldest-known Tarot decks still in existence. Of its seventy-four cards, twenty-six are housed at the Academy of Carrara in Bergamo, Italy; thirteen are owned by a private collector in Bergamo; and thirty-five are located in the Pierpont-Morgan Library in New York.

The fact that the Visconti-Sforza deck has endured relatively unscathed indicates that it probably was not used very much. Holes punched in the top suggest that the cards might have been hung on walls for decorative display. While the cards are not numbered, and therefore it is impossible to know with

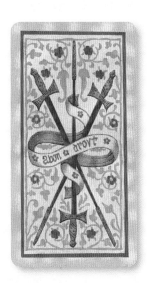

certainty that this deck included the four missing standard cards—the Devil, Tower, Three of Swords (left), and Knight of Coins—it is assumed that it did, and to complete the deck replicated in this kit, these four cards have been re-created in a style consistent with the existing cards.

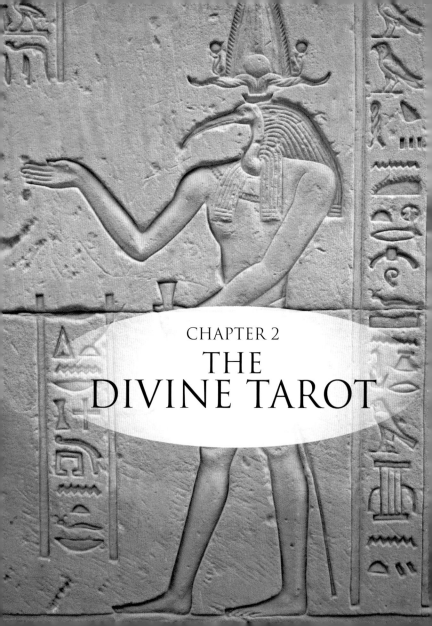

CHAPTER 2
THE
DIVINE TAROT

"If one heard it announced that there still exists in our days a work of the ancient Egyptians, one of their books that had escaped the flames that devoured their magnificent libraries, and that contained in a pure form their doctrines concerning interesting subjects, everyone would without doubt be eager to come to know so precious and so remarkable a book."

So stated the eighteenth-century French author Antoine Court de Gébelin who, on playing a game of Tarot for the first time, became so enthralled with the images he saw on the cards that he formulated a theory to explain their origin. He believed that all the wisdom of ancient Egypt was suddenly revealed to him through the Tarot cards. In the images, he saw the symbols

Opposite page: *The Egyptian god Thoth*

of the great enchantress Isis, goddess of rebirth and mother of all things. He also discerned messages from Thoth, the Egyptian god who discovered the natural laws governing all aspects of human happiness. It is because de Gébelin had already extensively studied the occult that he was able to recognize these glimmers of ancient mystical secrets in the cards.

De Gébelin's theory is not as wild as it might seem. The deck he used, called the Tarot of Marseilles, was a standardized deck popular in Europe at the time. Since all Tarot cards were first conceived in the early fifteenth century, when there was a renewed fervor for all things mystical, much of the cards' imagery reflected that interest.

De Gébelin expanded his theory in the eighth volume of his encyclopedia, *Le Monde primitif, analysé et comparé avec le monde moderne* (The Primeval World, Analyzed and Compared with the Modern World). For de Gébelin, the primeval world represented the golden age of humanity—an ideal civilization that was intellectually and spiritually superior to any civilization since. The inhabitants of this ideal world were followers of Thoth, who was reputed to have decoded the secrets of the universe and set them down in a repository of occult knowledge called the *Book of Thoth*. Legend has it that the *Book of Thoth* was kept in a temple where it was closely guarded by Egyptian priests, and according to de Gébelin, it was they who distilled the secrets in the book and codified them into the first Tarot images.

Four cards from a Tarot of Marseilles deck in the Bibliotheque Nationale in Paris

De Gébelin further theorized that the word *Tarot* meant the "royal road to wisdom," and was derived from two Egyptian words: *tar* ("road") and *rho* ("royal"). He also fleshed out his theories about the cards' parallels to Egyptian mythology. He pointed out, for example, that the triumphant figure on the Chariot card was the god Osiris, and the image featured on the Devil card was none other than the destructive Egyptian god Set. Finally, de Gébelin surmised that the cards had been brought to Europe by the Roma people, then called Gypsies because they were thought to have emigrated from Egypt.

To de Gébelin, the trump cards spelled out a creation story. Convinced that the cards had been reversed, he reordered the deck to fit his theory, starting with the World card, which for him represented Time. His deck ended with the Juggler (also called the Magician), who randomly and capriciously arranges and rearranges the divine elements, showing us that life is nothing more than a game of chance. De Gébelin also drew parallels between the first four suits and the four groups that made up the society in which he lived. He asserted that Swords stood for the nobility, Cups for the priesthood, Batons for farmers, and Coins for the merchant class.

After the Rosetta Stone had been deciphered in the early 1800s, it became obvious that there was nothing recorded in the Egyptian language to back up de Gébelin's theories about the Tarot's Egyptian origin. Nevertheless, Antoine Court de Gébelin's place in Tarot lore is secure. He was the first to link the Tarot with the occult and the first to realize that the

Tarot of Marseilles could be more than a mere instrument for amusement, setting the stage for future scholars to plumb the cards for intuitive meaning.

At around the same time as de Gébelin, Jean-Baptiste Alliette was developing his own theories about the Tarot. As a young man, he worked as a seed merchant and later, as a seller of antique prints. In his free time, he diligently studied Tarot decks, systematically developing and codifying his theories. Like de Gébelin, Alliette believed that the first Tarot deck had been invented in Egypt, and in 1788, he founded his own Tarot society, which he called the Society for Interpreting the Life of Thoth. He also studied astrology and numerology, and was the first to find ways to link them to the Tarot.

Although there is some evidence that Tarot cards had been used for divination during the Renaissance, it was Alliette, also known as Etteilla (his surname spelled backward), who was the first to create a Tarot deck specifically for this purpose. Etteilla is also credited with several other firsts: he wrote the first book on how to lay out Tarot cards and how to do a reading; coined the word *cartomancy*, the study of Tarot cards for use in divination; and became the first professional Tarot reader.

14.

FORCE MAJEURE.

14.

12.

LA PRUDENCE.

12.

2. 2.ᵉ Element. 1.ʳ Création.

ECLAIRCISSEMENT.

8.

15.

MALADIE.

15.

By 1791, Etteilla had created his own Tarot deck called the Grand Etteilla. For this deck, he changed the designs on many of the cards and reordered their sequence. Etteilla made other innovations as well. He numbered the cards from 1 to 78, with the Fool coming last. And although he included standard cards such as the Magician, Chariot, and Death, he also included an assortment of unfamiliar cards, such as Sky, Chaos, Prudence, and Fish. All of Etteilla's cards are labeled at both ends, so that they display different key words depending on whether images are upright or reversed. On specific cards in his deck, he included the signs of the zodiac and the four elements of air, water, earth, and fire.

Another of Etteilla's important contributions to cartomancy was his suggestion that a Tarot card could influence the interpretation of a reading depending on the card's relation to the other cards around it and how they all came together to form a whole. Etteilla's enthusiasm for cartomancy knew no bounds. In fact, from time to time, Etteilla actually used all seventy-eight cards to create the largest Tarot spread ever devised. He called this grand configuration the Great Figure of Destiny.

Opposite page: *Four cards from a nineteenth-century version of the Etteilla Tarot deck*

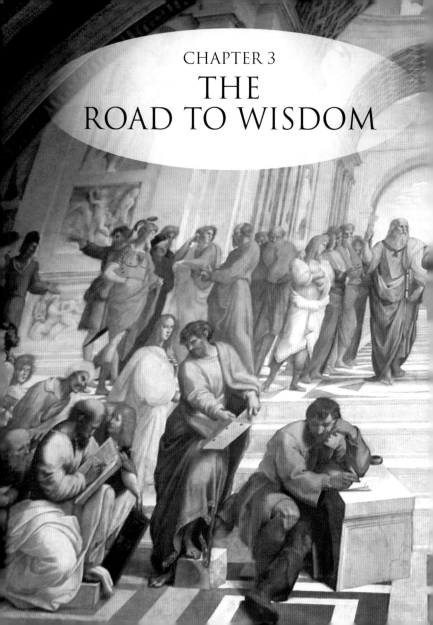

CHAPTER 3
THE
ROAD TO WISDOM

We know now that the first Tarot playing cards were created not in Egypt, but in fifteenth-century Milan at the dawn of the Renaissance. A characteristic of this intellectually vibrant era was the distillation and synthesis of a rich variety of cultural and spiritual traditions into a unified whole. In Italy, the wealth of ideas deriving from multiple schools of thought converged to make it a hotbed of creative activity.

This chapter will briefly summarize several of these strains of thought, including the revived philosophies of ancient Greece, Rome, and Egypt. After identifying representations of these ideas in the imagery of the Visconti-Sforza cards, it should be evident that this deck is much more than an assortment of playing cards, and that, although the first Tarot deck created expressly for divination was not made until the eighteenth century, the richness of the symbolism in the Visconti-Sforza deck makes it an ideal vehicle for divination and self-exploration.

Previous page: *Reverence for classical thought is beautifully embodied in this fresco that was painted for Pope Julius II by Raphael between 1509 and 1511.*

Although the Tarot did not originate in Egypt, some of the concepts expressed in it did. Those concepts, derived from a philosophical school of thought known as Hermeticsm, were first recorded in a collection of ancient texts now called the *Hermetica*.

Written in the second and third centuries, the texts were an amalgam of mythology, philosophy, astrology, and the magical arts, that despite their having been written by different authors, were said to have emanated directly from the mythical Thoth. A century later, after Alexander the Great conquered Egypt in 334, the Greeks adopted Thoth as their own, renaming him Hermes Trismegistus, which explains why the mystical philosophy associated with an Egyptian god is named for a Greek one. In the Egyptian texts, the name Thoth was usually followed by the phrase "great, great, great." To show that Hermes was identical to Thoth, the Greeks added *Trismegistus*, which means "thrice great," to the new name.

Hermeticism sought to answer the quintessential human dilemma—how to overcome death and attain immortality. Based on the idea that everyone possesses an immortal soul trapped within a mortal body, followers of Hermeticism believed that it was possible to become immortal and to join the Creator in the celestial realm above the planets. While arduous, the blueprint offered by the *Hermetica* for achieving immortality included meditation and ritual combined with several other spiritual and magical practices.

"Look, listen, and understand. Thou see'est the seven spheres of all life. Through them is accomplished the fall and ascent of souls."

—The Vision, The Second Book of the *Hermetica*

THE VISION

During the Renaissance, elements contained in the *Hermetica* would find new expression in the art of the Visconti-Sforza Tarot deck and later on, in the Tarot of Marseilles. A look at the mythology associated with Hermetic thought will help identify those elements.

In the first book of the *Hermetica*, we learn that Hermes received a divine revelation through which he learned everything there is to know. He found out, for example, that the Creator had shone celestial light into the four elements of earth, air, fire, and water to mold Earth and the seven planets. To ancient astronomers, the sun and moon were considered planets along with Mercury, Venus, Mars, Jupiter, and Saturn. All seven, along with the stars, circled Earth, which was stationary.

The Creator also revealed to Hermes how the first person came into being. He was told that God created the first person in his and her own image; and since that person was a reflection of God, the newly created entity was of dual gender and breathtakingly beautiful. The Creator allowed the first person to descend to the realm of the planets where all seven were stunned by the entity's splendor. Earth fell in love as well and gifted the bisexual being with a body, while the seven planets, hoping to keep the first person all to themselves, bestowed on it seven less attractive gifts—the vices of gluttony, cunning, lust, arrogance, audacity, greed, and falsehood.

Above: *The Lord Creating the Sun and Moon,* by Federico Zuccaro, 1566–69

The planets' wish to keep the entity to themselves did not pan out. The Creator split the first person in two, forming a man and a woman whose mission was to populate Earth. But perfect happiness would be forever out of their reach because Destiny had condemned humanity to suffer the pain of death. Each mortal body, however, contained a soul that was eternal. After death, in order to achieve unity with the divine Creator, the soul would have to climb the ladder of planets, shedding its vices along the way. This journey of purification would continue until at last the soul reached the heavenly realm.

It is this journey—the process of reunification with the divine—that is echoed symbolically in the images on the trumps. The seven heavenly bodies, including the five planets, the sun, and the moon, are the basis for mystical associations with the number seven and are reflected in the arrangement of the twenty-one hierarchical trumps, which are divided

"Then, being naked of all the accumulations of the seven Rings, the soul comes to the Eighth Sphere."

—Hermes Trismegistus

into three groups of seven. The first seven, from the Magician to the Chariot, represent worldly figures. The second group, from Justice to Temperance, depicts spiritual growth through suffering and acceptance of the Virtues. The third group, from the Devil to the World, traces the soul's journey to the heavenly realm, or enlightenment.

The Hermetic Cosmos

"Have you ever sensed that our soul is immortal and never dies?"

—Plato, *The Republic*

THE PATH TO ENLIGHTENMENT

To Plato, the Greek philosopher who lived in the third century BCE, the impermanence of the body coupled with a human being's capacity for abstract thought indicated that there was something beyond the world of matter—something that transcended mere flesh and bone. That ineffable something was the soul. If so many of the qualities that make up the soul can't be seen, Plato reasoned, then they must be part of something larger, a kind of a spiritual unity that he called the One. And after death, he thought, it was the task of every soul to reunite with the One. In his masterpiece, *The Republic*, Plato creates an allegory in which humanity is condemned to a life of darkness in a cave deep within the earth. In that world, life is nothing but an illusion. Plato's hero, a lover of truth, longs for sunlight and does not give up until, drawn upward by the light, he has risen to the mouth of the cave and finds ultimate enlightenment.

Plato's philosophy of the soul was modified in the third century CE to include the concept of God. This updated version, called Neoplatonism, incorporated diverse strains of religious thought and included biblical references as well as mysticism. The link between truth and light remained a defining concept. Neoplatonism flourished during the Renaissance, and reflections of it can be seen in the Tarot. It is not coincidental that three of the highest trumps in the Visconti-Sforza deck are the Star, Moon, and Sun. This hierarchical progression ends with the World card (right), which bears an image of the New Jerusalem, the embodiment of Heaven as set forth in the book of Revelation.

THE ALCHEMICAL LINK

The Hermetic trend that was revived during the Renaissance incorporated a fascination with the occult and the magical arts, including alchemy. The most famous alchemical text is *The Emerald Tablet*, which according to legend, was written by Hermes Trismegistus himself. The study of alchemy, the ancient science of turning base metals into gold, spread throughout Western Europe during the Middle Ages and continued throughout the Renaissance. Before exploring the link between alchemy and the Tarot, it helps to understand some of alchemy's basic principles.

Alchemy is a philosophy whose major tenet is, to quote Tarot scholar Robert M. Place, "that all things are alive, including rocks and minerals, and all share a common purpose: to evolve

"Alchemy is the art that separates what is useful from what is not by transforming it into its ultimate matter and essence."

—Philippus Aureolus Paracelsus

into their highest state of being." *The Emerald Tablet* gives a detailed account of transmutation, the alchemical process of change. In this belief system, a plant's highest form is a rose, a metal's is gold, and a human's is wisdom. To attain their highest form, substances must be cleansed of all impurities.

Although alchemists believed that, over time, lead would transmute into gold, they sought to speed up the process. To that end, they spent their lives searching for the catalyst that would perform this miracle of transmutation without the intervening steps. They called their quest the *Magnum Opus*, Latin for the "Great Work," and the magical substance they sought, the philosopher's stone, or *Anima Mundi*, "World Soul."

The Alchemist, *a fresco from "The Working World" cycle, by Nicolo Miretto and Stefano da Ferrara, after Giotto, ca. 1450*

> "Alchemy is the art of manipulating life, and consciousness in matter, to help it evolve, or to solve problems of inner disharmonies."

—Jean Dubuis

SPIRITUAL GOLD

Although practitioners of the Magnus Opus continued to search for the philosopher's stone, for some, the focus became more spiritual than material. For them, the overriding quest was to find a way to perfect the human soul through a mystical transformation. To achieve this goal, they explored dreams, visions, and symbols. The trumps tell the story of a symbolic journey of spiritual ascent that reflects that basic philosophy.

On the Visconti-Sforza Wheel of Fortune card (opposite page), a blindfolded Fortune spins her wheel, surrounded by four figures, each with a barely visible scroll nearby. The scroll by the left-hand figure reads *Regnabo* ("I shall reign"), the one by the top figure, *Regno* ("I am reigning"), and the

one by the right-hand figure, *Regnavi* ("I have reigned"). All are balanced on the back of a destitute but resigned old man whose scroll reads *Sum sino regno* ("I am without reign"). The message couldn't be clearer. The pursuit of fame and fortune is a base instinct (lead). By divesting oneself of unrestrained ambition, one can achieve transformation and become one step closer to enlightenment (gold).

"Only by discovering alchemy have I clearly understood that the Unconscious is a process and that ego's rapports with the unconscious and his contents initiate an evolution, more precisely a real metamorphosis of the psyche."

—Carl Jung

MODERN INTERPRETATIONS

The work of Swiss psychologist Carl Jung established the powerful role that images play in the life of the mind. In comparing the lore of disparate cultures throughout the ages, he observed that the images swirling in the unconscious were remarkably similar and reflected universal themes. Jung called these images archetypes. Among them were the wise old person, the hero, the trickster, the mother, and the innocent child. It is probably not coincidental that more than a few examples of these archetypal images make an appearance in the Tarot.

In his writings, Jung gave examples of belief systems that incorporate such archetypes, including alchemy and yoga, and noted, "It also seems as if the set of pictures in the Tarot cards were distantly descended from the archetypes of

transformation." For Tarot expert Cynthia Giles, Jung's sentence "bestowed a certain legitimacy to the notion of personal growth through the study of Tarot." Few would dispute the value of plumbing our dreams to uncover hidden motivations and buried emotions. Jung confirmed the importance of myth, fables, dreams, and folk tales in uncovering hidden motivations and buried emotions. Through their symbolism, Tarot cards can perform precisely this function, with the distinction that they do so while we are awake.

In the Visconti-Sforza Tarot deck, Il Tempo *("Time"), also called the Hermit, is the personification of the wise old person.*

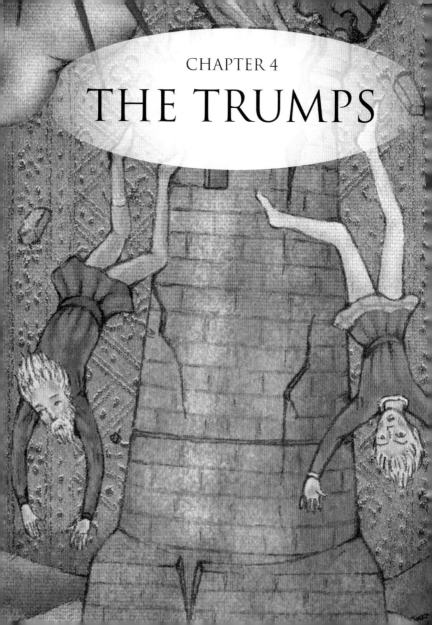

CHAPTER 4
THE TRUMPS

> "The true Tarot is symbolism;
> it speaks no other language and
> offers no other signs."

—Arthur E. Waite, *Soul Symbols*

Archival documents show that Marziano da Tortona, astrologer and card designer, once asked his client Duke Filippo Visconti if it was appropriate for a serious and virtuous man to spend time playing a card game. Visconti answered that if the game was virtuous in the philosophy that it represented, it would indeed be a worthwhile pursuit. This historical anecdote reinforces the view held by Renaissance scholars that all works of art, even for games, were meant to express meaningful ideas through metaphor and allegory.

Opposite page: *A detail of the re-created Tower card in the Visconti-Sforza deck*

The Visconti-Sforza Tarot deck is a perfect example of this tradition. Some have suggested that when viewed as three chapters of a story, Tarot trump cards are allegories for Plato's theory of the three-part soul: the Soul of Appetite, the Soul of Will, and the Soul of Reason. For Plato, it was necessary to integrate the three Soul Centers by purifying them with virtues. This allegory is accomplished in the Tarot by progressing from the lowest trump to the highest. The first seven Tarot trumps in the hierarchy correspond to the Soul of Appetite and are purified through the virtue of Temperance. The second set corresponds to the Soul of Will, symbolized by the desire for power and status. The Soul of Will is purified through the virtue of Fortitude, or Strength.

The last seven trumps represent the Soul of Reason's struggle to gain control of the Soul of Will, irrational impulses personified by the Devil. Once these three aspects of the soul have been purified, the soul can function as one, Justice can reign, and the soul is free to ascend higher and higher toward celestial bodies of increasing brightness (the Star, the Moon, the Sun) until at last, it reaches its Neoplatonic home in Heaven, represented by the World card.

You may have heard or seen the term *Major Arcana* used to refer to trump cards in other Tarot decks. But as it was coined over four hundred years after the first Tarot cards were created, the term does not apply to the Visconti-Sforza trumps. Each trump in this deck will be defined by two names: its original Italian name and the name most recognizable to the modern Tarot reader. There are twenty-two trump cards in this fifth suit, twenty-one of which, although not numbered, have a set sequence. The twenty-second card, the Fool, does not have a fixed place in the hierarchy of the trumps, and can be either first (as in *The Golden Tarot*) or last.

In this chapter, we will explore the symbolic imagery of the trumps in the Visconti-Sforza deck. These cards represent, through archetypes, all the joys and sorrows that an individual can experience over a lifetime. How one responds to the imagery offers a way of gaining insight into one's own emotions and patterns of thought.

THE FOOL
IL MATTO

This well-known character from the Renaissance was originally called *Il Matto*, "The Madman." He wears tattered clothing, long socks with the feet worn away, and feathers protruding from his wild hair— all indications that the figure is ill-prepared for life and must learn every lesson through trial and error. Representing the archetype of innocence, the Fool is the proverbial babe in the woods who has yet to learn lessons through experience. Though clueless, he is at the very beginning of his journey to attain wisdom.

Upright: Innocence; auspicious start of new adventures and opportunities; enthusiastic willingness to make a fool of oneself to reach one's Higher Self

Reversed: Faulty choices and bad decision making are in effect or loom ahead

THE GOLDEN TAROT

THE MAGICIAN
IL BAGATELLA

The first trump in the hierarchy, the Magician is the first guide on the quest for wisdom. His clothing indicates that he is most likely a trickster or carnival king, another popular figure from the triumphs. In Italian, *Il Bagatella* means "something of little importance." The Magician represents the Soul of Appetite, the lowest rung on the ladder to self-actualization. He is perched on an elaborately decorated trunk before a stark table on which are arranged a knife, a cup, two coins, and a large covered dish. His right hand rests on the covered dish, and in his left hand, he holds a rod. Symbolically, the cup represents a benign motive; the knife, a clear plan; the rod, enthusiasm; and the coins, all that is practical. And who knows what lies hidden in the trunk? Out of these elements, anything and everything is possible.

Upright: An auspicious card for beginning something new; indicates imagination, originality, skill that can be used for good or ill

Reversed: Refusal to commit; seeking an easy way out; weakness

HIGH PRIESTESS
LA PAPESSA

Based on her extensive research, Tarot scholar Gertrude Moakley has suggested that the image on this card, originally called *La Papessa* ("The Popess") in Italian, is of Sister Manfreda, a relative of the Visconti family and member of a small heretical sect called the Guglielmites. This sect elected Sister Manfreda as their pope, in accordance with their belief that the male-dominated papacy was soon to be replaced by a line of female popes. The High Priestess sits on a throne wearing a triple crown, the symbol of papal authority. As High Priestess, she represents power, a temporal quality that is ruled by the Soul of Appetite. But she is also symbolic of the Soul of Will harnessed to achieve lofty pursuits and fearlessly turn seemingly out-of-reach goals into reality.

Upright: Good judgment; sound intuition; a good card to show spiritual evolution; serene wisdom; platonic love; introspection; deep, hidden emotion

Reversed: Inability to harness spirituality; selfishness; shallowness

The Golden Tarot

THE EMPRESS
L'IMPERATRICE

In her right hand, the Empress holds a scepter and in her left, a shield emblazoned with a black eagle, the heraldic device of the Holy Roman Emperor and his wife. This is the first card to combine the heraldic devices of both the Visconti and Sforza families. The Empress wears a robe on which are etched three interlaced diamond rings that represent the Sforza family, and on her head, she wears the Visconti crown. As the earth mother archetype, the Empress embodies female attractiveness and fertility. Combined with her crown, scepter, and shield, she is the personification of feminine power.

Upright: Feminine power; fertility; female charm; practicality; decisiveness; maternal love; material wealth

Reversed: Infertility; infidelity; anxiety

THE EMPEROR
L'IMPERADORE

As a symbol of his authority, the imperial globe is prominently displayed in the palm of the Emperor's hand. Heraldic devices of both families are reflected in his robe, including the Sforza triple rings and the Visconti crown. On his crown can be seen the Holy Roman Emperor's coat of arms, the imperial eagle. The Emperor's flowing white beard, an archetype of ancient wisdom, unites with his crown, scepter, and imperial globe to create a figure that epitomizes masculine power.

Upright: Stability; worldly power; control of one's own ego; may also suggest an encounter with the law or someone in a position of authority; a promise of victory

Reversed: A warning not to trust someone who wields power over you; lack of control; petty emotion; failure due to an inability to focus

THE POPE
IL PAPA

In real life, the Pope possesses the right to crown the Emperor, and his position in the trump story appropriately places him above the other rulers. The Pope's right hand is raised in a sign of benediction, and in his left hand, he holds the papal cross. He wears the three-tiered crown that symbolizes papal authority and represents the unity of mind, body, and spirit. His white beard is an archetype for wisdom, while his white tunic represents purity of soul. Together, the robe, crown, and cross stand for ceremony and ritual, imparting historical significance and gravitas to his bearing. In spite of the Pope's lofty title, all power is temporal, symbolized by the Pope's position in the trumps.

Upright: Spirituality; compassion; forgiveness; constrained thinking; conformity

Reversed: Vulnerability; foolish generosity; nonconformity; rejection of orthodox doctrine; in the extreme, gullibility as in adherence to a cult

THE LOVERS
L'AMORE

It is widely believed that the clothed figures on this card are Francesco Sforza and Bianca Maria Visconti. The card's Italian name *L'Amore* ("Love"), the absence of facial expression, and the sparseness of detail indicate that, in this deck, the actual subject is Love itself and not the Lovers. Presided over by a winged Cupid, the Lovers' pose was inspired by standard betrothal portraits, such as those that appeared on wedding plates and other forms of wedding memorabilia at the time. Cupid stands above the Lovers on a pedestal, showing that he is more powerful than they are. He wears a blindfold to indicate the randomness of his arrows and the inexplicable reasons why people fall in love. During the Renaissance, Cupid was considered a troublesome type who personified the Soul of Appetite and whose lust needed to be harnessed in the institution of marriage.

Upright: Harmony; love; trust; honor; joy; the fulfillment of desires; a new relationship or a new stage of an existing one

Reversed: Fickleness; lack of trust

THE CHARIOT
IL CARRO TRIUMPHALE

No card exemplifies the triumph parades' influence on the
Tarot more than the Chariot trump, originally called *Il Carro
Triumphale* ("the Triumphal Chariot"). Here, Bianca Maria
personifies Laura, the protagonist of Petrarch's *I Trionfi*.
As driver of the chariot, Laura displays multiple symbols
of authority, including the golden crown on her head, the
scepter carried in one hand, and the imperial globe held in the
other. Enacting the Neoplatonic quest for immortality, Laura
manifests as archetype for the hero. As such, she must exert her
will over the winged horses—one of which represents the Soul
of Appetite and the other, the Soul of Will—as she guides the
entire chariot/soul toward enlightenment.

Upright: Conflict; turbulence; imminent voyage or journey;
internal struggle to keep physical and mental powers in balance;
search for truth and harmony

Reversed: Failure; defeat

JUSTICE
LA JUSTICIA

Justice leads the second set of trumps, and it is this virtue's mission to challenge the Soul of Will. Grasping the scales of justice, an archetype for fairness and balance, in her left hand, and displaying a double-edged sword in her right hand, Justice indicates that she is more than up to the task. For visual interest and in conformance with the conventions of the day, another drama plays out on this trump. Above Justice, as if in a dream or in her imagination, an armored knight on a white stallion gallops across the golden arch framing her crown. He is brandishing his sword, prepared to defend her and her cause, in compliance with the first rule of chivalry—to defend that which is fair and just. The rays of the sun beam down benignly from both the left and right top corners of the card.

Upright: Fairness; balance; honor; impartiality; good intentions; equilibrium and poise; someone who is kind and appreciates consideration from others

Reversed: Bigotry; false accusations; abuse; intolerance

THE HERMIT
IL TEMPO

The Hermit, his long flowing beard an archetype for wisdom, holds a rod or walking stick in his left hand and an hourglass in his right. He contemplates the hourglass, aware that time is passing quickly. His sumptuous two-tiered, gold-trimmed fur hat indicates that he is man of some wealth. This image of the old man as the personification of Time (*Il Tempo*) owes its genesis to the character of Time as illustrated in the pages of Petrarch's *I Trionfi*, which in turn was derived from classical depictions of Saturn, the god of time, who was also pictured as a hunchbacked old man. An interesting sidelight in interpreting the card's symbolism is that, in Italy, charms of hunchbacks are worn for good luck.

Upright: A warning to take stock of one's actions to ensure that they are meaningful before it is too late; watchfulness; circumspection

Reversed: Impulsiveness; foolish haste; failure brought about by a lack of attention

THE WHEEL OF FORTUNE
LA RUOTA DELLA FORTUNA

The Wheel of Fortune, also discussed on pages 40–41, is associated with time and the physical, temporal world, in which nothing stays the same. Blindfolded Fortuna, as the embodiment of indifference, is impervious to the fates of those around her. The figures at the top and left of Fortuna sport donkey ears, and the figure on the right has a tail. An old man in tattered clothing supports them all. This card indicates that life is change. If it's in an upright position, all is rosy; reversed, not so much.

Upright: Destiny; coming to the end of a problem; whether the outcome is good or bad will depend upon the cards nearest to it

Reversed: Interruption; reversal of fortune; repeated bad luck due to inability to learn from experience

THE GOLDEN TAROT

STRENGTH
LA FORTEZZA

The art style of this card indicates that it was not painted by
Bonifacio Bembo. The features of the young man's face are
not as refined as those of the figures on the preceding trump
cards and were most likely painted by an artist named Antonio
Cicognara. Strength, as personified by the figure of Hercules,
is the discipline necessary for the soul to complete its journey.
The lion stands for the inflated ego that seeks fame and fortune
above all else. Strength's power springs from courage, a word
derived from the Latin root *cor*, which means "heart." Strength,
then, is the quality needed to tame man's lust for power.

Upright: Physical strength; mind over matter; self-discipline;
determination; heroism

Reversed: Pettiness; impotence; abuse of power

THE HANGED MAN
IL TRADITORE

The figure on the card hangs upside down, tethered by his left ankle to a gallows. The similarity between his face and the male figure in the Lovers card indicates that he is probably a member of the Visconti-Sforza family. The Hanged Man, *Il Traditore* ("The Traitor") in Italian, would have been an instantly recognizable figure in fifteenth-century Italy because hanging upside down was the punishment for traitors. Political figures were sometimes depicted hanging upside down as a form of derision. The Hanged Man represents pain and the loss of ego necessary for the soul to complete its spiritual quest.

Upright: Suffering and shame; loss of ego, self-esteem, material wealth; a period of limbo between significant events; suspension of action; transition; change of course; sacrifice; repentance

Reversed: Useless sacrifice; failure to give what's needed; egotism

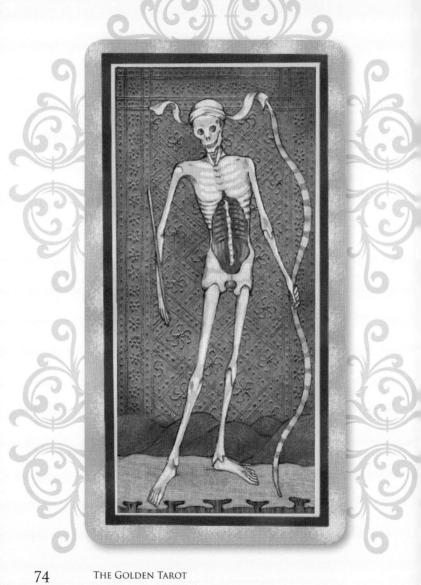

THE GOLDEN TAROT

DEATH
LA MORTE

This eerily animated skeleton was a starring figure in an allegorical theme called the *Dance of Death*, created in response to a plague that decimated the population in the fourteenth century. Death holds a bow in its left hand and an arrow in its right. Its piercing eyes stare menacingly out of deep, shadowed eye sockets. We have seen that Strength, having triumphed over unrestrained ambition, has been trumped by the pain and suffering of the Hanged Man and now, by Death. But it's obvious from Death's position in this allegory that all is not lost; there are many more trump cards left in the deck.

Upright: Transformation; endings—of a relationship, a job, income—which are necessary before one can begin again; in the extreme, impending illness or death

Reversed: Crippling fear of change

TEMPERANCE
LA TEMPERANZA

Temperance is the last of the cardinal virtues illustrated in the trumps. She is the virtue that leads to balance, health, and harmony. She achieves her goal not by denying appetites and emotions but by keeping them in check. Moderation is the key. Temperance soothes the soul and eases the urge to rail at the unfairness of life. She is about to pour liquid from one ornate jug to another as she stands at the edge of a precipice, metaphorically blending the interior world of the psyche with the exterior physical world of appetite, the perfect state needed to achieve peace of mind. The style of the painting indicates that the figure was executed by an artist other than Bonifacio Bembo, most likely Antonio Cicognara, the same artist who is thought to have painted Strength.

Upright: Nurturing and health; self-control without denial; moderation and balance in all things

Reversed: Disharmony; conflicts of interest

THE GOLDEN TAROT

THE DEVIL
EL DIAVOLO

Because this trump card is not among the surviving cards from the original Visconti-Sforza deck, it has been re-created picturing the Devil as it might have appeared in the fifteenth century. Fierce and menacing, this Devil is half man and half beast. It sports the wings of a bat, the horns of a ram, and the ears of an ass. A second face on its abdomen symbolizes the Soul of Appetite in its most out-of-control mode. Chained to the Devil's pedestal are two horned figures that represent man's baser animal instincts. The chains symbolize bondage to temporal, material pleasures. Fire erupts from the pedestal, a reminder of the pain that awaits those who fail to free themselves from the bondage of temporal desires and attend to matters of the soul.

Upright: Addiction; aggressive pursuit of earthly possessions; extreme craving for money and power; unprincipled; lacking in humor except at another's expense; violence; disaster

Reversed: Release from ties that bind; divorce; overcoming obstacles

THE TOWER
LA CASA DEL DIAVOLO

The sun sends a lightning bolt literally out of the blue, slicing off the top of the Tower, originally called *La Casa del Diavolo* ("The Devil's House") in Italian. The sun's impassive expression signals that calamity strikes randomly without regard to age or status. Two figures within, one an old man and the other a youthful female, come tumbling down, headfirst. The sturdy-looking stone tower is not the mighty fortress they might have imagined. All material is temporal and no match for unseen celestial forces. And all people, young and old, rich and poor, are destined to perish. Only the soul can endure. As was the case with the Devil card, the Tower has also been re-created in a fifteenth-century artistic style.

Upright: Sudden change; unforeseen catastrophe; collapse of old beliefs and doctrines; adversity; misery; financial setback; loss of relationship

Reversed: Continued subjugation; stuck in a rut; inability to change; imprisonment

THE STAR
LA STELLA

The Star begins the soul's mystical ascent through the heavenly bodies on its quest for spiritual enlightenment. In this card, the figure of a woman in blue raises a gold eight-pointed star above her head, signaling that heavenly radiance envelops her. She is the calm after the storm that destroyed the Tower. *Stelle* ("stars") is the last word of Dante's *Inferno*, appearing after the heroes emerge from Hell into a star-filled sky. The Star is the symbol for hope that Good will triumph over Evil. Art history experts have suggested that figure in this image might have been inspired by depictions of Urania, goddess of astronomy, one of the nine muses of Greek and Roman mythology. Urania's facial features, less refined than those of figures painted by Bonifacio Bembo, indicate that this trump, like Strength and Temperance, may have been painted by Antonio Cicognara.

Upright: Optimism; faith; an auspicious card in that it indicates that everything—work, love, family, efforts—are all in proper balance; very favorable outcome

Reversed: Disappointment; imbalance; pessimism

THE MOON
LA LUNA

In mythology, the moon is personified by Diana the Huntress, who is also the goddess of fertility. In the Moon card, she stands alone, separated from her twin, the sun god Apollo. She is shown holding up a crescent or "new" moon, indicating that her quest for eternity has not yet been achieved. Her rank in the trumps demonstrates that she is trumped by the World card that represents eternity. In Petrarch's poems, the Moon and Star must wait for Eternity to triumph over Time—which is why they are often depicted wearing sad faces. A manmade structure looms small and insignificant in the background, indicating the Moon's distance from temporal concerns. This is the fourth trump card that was executed by a different artist than Bonifacio Bembo. As it is similar in style to the Strength, Temperance, and Star cards, it is believed to have been painted by Antonio Cicognara.

Upright: Patience in anticipation; rest; respite; meditation; emergence of the unconscious

Reversed: Impatience

THE GOLDEN TAROT

THE SUN
IL SOLE

The Sun card shows a winged child or cherub, a popular figure in Renaissance art, known as a *putto* in Italian. His rounded form is more similar to the style of the cards attributed to Antonio Cicognara than to those cards known to be by Bonifacio Bembo. He stands on a floating blue cloud while holding up the sun, a favorite heraldic device of the Visconti-Sforza family. Here, the sun is shaped like the head of a god, meant to denote Apollo, the Greek and Roman sun god. Although the cliff's edge appears in the foreground, the child is nowhere near it. He wears a beaded necklace that might serve as a good luck charm. A thin scarf winds between his legs and around his shoulders. With the appearance of the Sun, the twins of mythology—the moon goddess (Diana) and the sun god (Apollo)—are united, representing completion and the balancing of opposites, light and dark, day and night, movement and rest. Psychologically, their union can also represent the merging of the conscious and unconscious mind, the perfect state according to Jung.

Upright: The ideal in all things including health; perfect harmony and unity; a balance between the masculine and feminine that signifies deepening love; fame; pleasure; satisfaction

Reversed: Loneliness; clouded future; unhappy relationship

JUDGMENT
L'ANGELO

This card was called *L'Angelo*, "The Angel," when it was first created. A divine, god-like figure presides over angels who are summoning the figures below with their trumpets. At the bottom of the card, two figures, representing Bianca Maria Visconti and Francesco Sforza, are seated in a coffin. Between them reposes an old man who seems to be at the bottom of the tomb, indicating that though he may have predeceased them, he is also heaven bound. As they are about to embark on their journey to heaven, the figures gaze joyfully at the celestial beings above. In addition to this biblical interpretation of the Last Judgment, the mystical quest is almost complete as the soul triumphs over Death with the promise of eternal life.

Upright: Atonement; accountability; rejuvenation and healing

Reversed: Indecision; spiritual emptiness; addiction

THE GOLDEN TAROT

THE WORLD
IL MONDO

This is the sixth and final card in Visconti-Sforza deck that has been attributed to Antonio Cicognara. Together, two putti hold up a globe, a symbolic representation of heaven where the redeemed, seen in the Judgment card, will make their new home. The World card is also symbolic of the enlightenment of eternity. The soul, having defeated Death and Time, has joined with the One to achieve immortality. Within the globe is a shining a castle on a hill. Protected by a moat, the castle is a metaphor for the New Jerusalem promised in the book of Revelation. The sky is blue and cloudless, and the angelic putti are safe, symbolically protected by the scarves draped around their shoulders.

Upright: Extremely auspicious card; perfect completion; clear sailing; inner happiness

Reversed: Lack of vision; failure to complete what is started; disappointment

CHAPTER 5
THE FOUR SUITS

Suit	Association	Class	Element	Astrological Sign
Cups	Joy	Clergy	Water	Scorpio
Swords	Sorrow	Nobility	Air	Aquarius
Batons	Country	Peasants	Fire	Leo
Coins	Money	Merchants	Earth	Taurus

Although the cards in the first four suits of the Visconti-Sforza Tarot deck lack the rich, spiritual imagery and archetypes that characterize the trump cards in the fifth suit, they are certainly not devoid of meaning. Based on the repetitions of the suit symbols, they are still very informative and subject to interpretation. And while they are not meant to guide you on a spiritual path, they do impart valuable information about personality and mood. After you have studied these cards extensively and become well-versed in their meanings, you will develop your own intuitive ideas about how they can contribute to a layout.

The names of the four suits are Cups, Swords, Coins, and Batons. Each suit is made up of fourteen cards: ten numerical cards, often referred to as pips, and four court cards, the King, Queen, Knight, and Knave. As noted in chapter two, these four suits mirror the four classes of Medieval and Renaissance society: the clergy, the nobility, the merchants, and the peasants. They also correspond to the four elements of water, air, earth, and fire, and reflect the personality traits associated with each. These suits have been linked with astrological signs as well.

THE CUPS SUIT

This is a lighthearted suit that represents joy. Cups cards are rarely negative and often function as a mitigating factor when situated near negative cards in a layout. The Cups can also represent the unconscious. It is interesting to note that the Two of Cups bears the phrase *amor mio* ("my love") and the Four of Cups, the Visconti insignia, *à bon droyt* ("with good [there is] right.").

Ace of Cups

The "cup" on this card is a hexagonal fountain resembling a baptismal font or perhaps a chalice suggestive of the Holy Grail.

Upright: An auspicious card indicating luxury, affluence, fulfillment, and joy

Reversed: Unreciprocated affection; sterility; marred happiness

Two of Cups

Upright: Cooperative relationships of all kinds; romantic love fulfilled; discernment; altruistic impulses

Reversed: Divorce; separation; secrecy; complacency; an inability to connect

Three of Cups

Upright: Completion; healing; compromise; may also indicate an imminent celebration, holiday gathering, and/or family reunion

Reversed: Hedonistic pleasure; overindulgence; ingratitude

Four of Cups

Upright: Introspection; the need to gain some perspective after an intense period or siege of some kind; disillusionment and a resulting depletion of energy

Reversed: Suggests that one will learn new things, meet new people, and encounter new possibilities and experiences

Five of Cups

Upright: Regrets; flaws; imperfection; can also suggest a shallow relationship or an empty marriage

Reversed: Hints at a rosy future and hopeful attitude

Six of Cups

Upright: Faded dreams; extreme longing; a yearning for the past

Reversed: New beginnings; a bright future

Seven of Cups

Upright: Foolish notions; wishful thinking; dreaminess

Reversed: Smart choices; a goal nearly realized

Eight of Cups

Upright: Shyness; modesty; resignation; disappointment; an abandonment of effort

Reversed: Perseverance; a refusal to move on

Nine of Cups

Upright: The fulfillment of dreams; an auspicious card for material success and good health

Reversed: Errors and imperfection; superficiality and shallowness

Ten of Cups

Upright: An extremely auspicious card; romantic fulfillment; financial stability; a happy home; spiritual and emotional well-being; virtue; peace; honor; gratitude

Reversed: Disharmony; quarrelsome relationships; conflict; trouble

KNAVE OF CUPS

The Knave faces left (the direction of evil) and wears white gloves (a symbol of purity), which suggests good intentions in the face of malevolent forces. He holds a golden cup that, like all the court cards in this suit, is topped with a tall, gothic cover. His tunic is decorated with radiant suns, a heraldic device of the Viscontis. The contrast between the Knave's red and white stockings, if they intentionally reflect Renaissance symbolism, may represent a conflict between purity (white) and lust (red).

Upright: Caring; tender; artistic; very good communicator; might also indicate a pregnancy or birth

Reversed: Easily distracted; deviate; smooth talker; not to be trusted in love

KNIGHT OF CUPS

Mounted on a horse, the Knight of Cups wears a short, fur-trimmed coat of gold cloth imprinted with the Visconti sun. Beneath the coat, he wears a shirt of royal blue. The horse's right leg is raised, and its caparison and bridle bear the Visconti insignias.

Upright: Equal to meeting whatever comes one's way; concerned with love and romance; possesses psychic ability; an auspicious card indicating that an opportunity will soon present itself; possibly a marriage proposal

Reversed: Untrustworthy; selfish; scheming

QUEEN OF CUPS

Seated on a throne and
wearing a crown, the Queen
of Cups faces full front.
Her heavy-looking gold
gown is adorned with the
Visconti sun emblem. She
wears green gloves, a color
associated with the sacred in
Renaissance art. She holds
an ornate covered cup, or
chalice, in her right hand
and appears to be gesturing,
perhaps bestowing a
blessing, with her left.

Upright: Expansive;
kind; maternal; devoted;
adored; possesses the gift of
clairvoyance

Reversed: Unstable; demanding; dependent; punitive; given to
emotional outbursts

KING OF CUPS

Featured in profile, the
King of Cups wears the
ducal crown of Milan. His
fur-trimmed tunic bears the
Visconti heraldic device of a
sun with wavy and straight
rays. In his right hand, he
holds an ornate covered cup.

Upright: Considerate;
kind; dependable; possibly
religious; creative and fond
of the arts; concern for
others leads to charitable
pursuits

Reversed: Duplicitous;
shifty; scandalous

THE SWORDS SUIT

The Sword cards are associated with the element of air and as such, are linked to thinking and reason. In Renaissance portraiture, the sword was a symbol of Justice.

Ace of Swords

The Visconti motto *à bon droyt* appears on a scroll that wraps around the swords of the first five numerical cards, starting with the ace. This French phrase means "with good [there is] right."

Upright: Determination, initiative, and strength—all qualities that lead to success and lasting achievement

Reversed: Disaster; oppression; ferocious temper; humiliation; infertility

Two of Swords

Upright: A confrontation of equal forces leading to a stalemate; repressed emotion; inability to come to a decision

Reversed: Deceit; betrayal; lies; treachery

Three of Swords

The only pip card missing from the Visconti-Sforza deck, the Three of Swords was re-created in a style similar to that of the other Swords pips.

Upright: Disappointment; heartache; desolation; despair; an imminent separation; possible deferral of plans

Reversed: Absence; loss; rejection; regret

Four of Swords

Upright: Rejuvenation; recovery from prior adversity; signifies that it's time to slow down; a need for solitary pursuits such as meditation; temporary isolation; exile; reprieve

Reversed: An urge to keep going; increased stress

Five of Swords

Upright: Gain at the expense of others; betrayal and misplaced trust

Reversed: Cloudy outlook; uncertainty; weakness

Six of Swords

Upright: Stability and smooth sailing; travel and/or relocation; the overcoming of adversity

Reversed: Stasis; impasse; old patterns of behavior; inability to make progress

Seven of Swords

Upright: A contradictory card, it may signify deceit and trickery or stand for creative risk; one might fail by overplaying one's hand or triumph by using one's wits

Reversed: Uncertainty; justice prevails when bad behavior gets punished

Eight of Swords

Upright: Temporary isolation; imprisonment; confinement due to illness; inhibitions; depression; lethargy

Reversed: Release; freedom; light at the end of the tunnel

Nine of Swords

Upright: Sometimes referred to as "the nightmare card" because it represents, worry, anxiety, and a troubled mental state; hopelessness; misery

Reversed: Shame; scandal; gossip

Ten of Swords

Upright: Letting go of the past in the interest of healing and personal growth—a process that can bring with it emotional anguish; forgiveness

Reversed: Temporary gain; fleeting success; slightly improving circumstances

KNAVE OF SWORDS

The Knave of Swords is fully armored and sports a peacock-feathered hat. He poses gracefully and holds his sword in his right hand with the point resting non-threateningly on the ground.

Upright: Mental risk-taker, concerned with intellectual ideas; strongly perceptive; insightful; capable of uncovering hidden meanings; discreet; alert; adaptable; would make a good spy. Card might indicate that important information or document is on its way; hints at a possible conflict.

Reversed: An impostor; unable to cope with unforeseen forces; depending on surrounding cards, could indicate impending illness

KNIGHT OF SWORDS

The Knight of Swords sits astride an armored white horse, a symbol of invincibility. Like the Knave of Swords, the Knight is clad in full armor and sports a hat covered in peacock feathers, which were a symbol of pride during the Renaissance. The Knight is pictured in profile facing left (the direction of evil) and carrying a raised sword in his right hand. His dignified, composed bearing indicates that he can always be depended on to fight the good fight but should not be called upon to engage in trivial causes.

Upright: Gallantry and heroism; can also signal sudden change and risk taking

Reversed: Passive; irresponsible; conceited

QUEEN OF SWORDS

Seated in profile, the Queen wears a crown, gauntlets, and armor on her forearms and elbows. She is clothed in white, a symbol of purity; at Italian universities during the Renaissance, white was also a symbol of the humanities. In her right hand, she holds a sword that rests over her shoulder, and her left hand is raised as if in a greeting.

Upright: Smart; perceptive; self-contained; may have known happiness at one time but is now full of sorrow; harsh disciplinarian; may be unable to show affection. This card signifies fleeting happiness.

Reversed: Bigoted; deceitful; shirks responsibility; neglects loved ones

KING OF SWORDS

Like the figures in the other three court cards in this suit, the King of Swords wears armor and carries a large sword. He is the only king in the four suits to have a shield. The shield is adorned with a haloed lion holding a book, an emblem of Venice, a city that was once under the protection of the Sforzas.

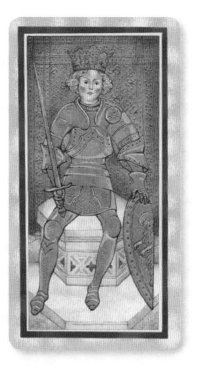

Upright: Someone in a position of authority who has reached the pinnacle of a profession such the law, the military, or higher education; analytic; filled with bright ideas and innovative plans

Reversed: Selfish; domineering; dangerous

THE BATONS SUIT

The associations of this suit with the country and farming have broadened to accommodate modern interpretations. Today, the suit is concerned with leadership, innovation, and communication as they relate to business matters.

Ace of Batons

As with the Swords suit, the Visconti motto *à bon droyt* (French for "with good [there is] right") appears on a scroll that, here, wraps around the batons on the first five numerical cards.

Upright: An auspicious card for beginning something new; successfully completed mission; good luck; prosperity

Reversed: Uncertain results; thwarted ambition; truncated plans

Two of Batons

Upright: Mature dominant character; high energy; optimism; goals realized through determination and hard work

Reversed: Sorrow; adversity; unforeseen defeat

Three of Batons

Upright: Strength; business skills; practical street smarts

Reversed: Unrealistic expectations; wasted dreams; a warning against helpers with ulterior motives

Four of Batons

Upright: The commemoration of important milestones; achievement and its rewards; recent affluence and serenity at home; commitment

Reversed: Uncertainty; delayed reward; a postponed celebration or a ruptured relationship

Five of Batons

Upright: Competition and struggle; may signal a need to stand up for oneself; implication that growth can only be achieved through overcoming obstacles

Reversed: Inaction; trivial quarrels; internal conflict; may be a warning against vacillation

Six of Batons

Upright: A harbinger of good news: victory has arrived and brought rewards for achievement along with it

Reversed: Fear; anxiety; betrayal

Seven of Batons

Upright: Success in the face of adversity; implies one will beat the odds

Reversed: Indecision; hesitancy; anxiety; failure to act due to worry

Eight of Batons

Upright: Swiftness; sudden advancement; impulsive decision making; perhaps a love at first sight

Reversed: Jealousy; family quarrels; delay; inertia

Nine of Batons

Upright: Goals that have been attained; a time to pause, reflect, and recover from the strain of too much effort; a need to let down defenses and relax

Reversed: Looming barriers and obstacles; perhaps an illness

Ten of Batons

Upright: A type A personality; the struggle toward a goal; responsibility taking its toll

Reversed: Pessimism; deceptive maneuvering

KNAVE OF BATONS

Seen from the back with his face turned in profile, the Knave of Batons wears a short fur-trimmed cape and holds a baton with ornate finials at either end. Beneath the stripes of the cape, the Visconti insignia of a brightly rayed sun is visible.

Upright: A trusted, loyal confidante; an enthusiastic extrovert brimming with new ideas; an auspicious card for romance and friendship

Reversed: Someone not to be trusted; a bearer of bad news; an indecisive nature

KNIGHT OF BATONS

A side view of the Knight of Batons showcases his horse's caparison with its escutcheons of shields and the Visconti heraldic device of a sun with shining rays. The Knight appears to be in full control of his spirited steed as it rears up on its hind legs.

Upright: A journey or a change of residence; enthusiasm; an adventurous spirit

Reversed: Friction; disturbance in or breakup of a relationship

QUEEN OF BATONS

The Queen sits on her throne in a relaxed, open position. She wears a softly flowing empire-style overdress with long, graceful sleeves. On the front of her dress, beneath the bodice, Visconti heraldic devices of a shining sun and a bird's nest can be seen.

Upright: Outgoing; loving; compassionate; graceful; charming; nonjudgmental; interested in others

Reversed: Fickle; jealous; deceitful; unfaithful; stubborn

KING OF BATONS

The King is seated on a hexagonal throne, which suggests that he is concerned with both temporal and spiritual matters. He faces full front with his legs crossed at the ankles. Like the Queen of Batons, he holds a scepter (symbol of authority) in his right hand and a royal baton in his left. His outfit bears the Visconti heraldic devices—a bird's nest and solar rays.

Upright: Confident; mature; successful; combines paternal instincts with an optimistic, generous nature

Reversed: Dogmatic; immature; impulsive

THE COINS SUIT

This suit represents the physical world of material pleasures. Once again, the Visconti motto *à bon droyt* (French for "with good [there is] right") appears on a scroll, this time on the second through fifth cards, appearing twice on the three and five cards. The coins themselves feature the heraldic sun of the Visconti family.

Ace of Coins

Upright: An auspicious card for new ventures and pursuing new opportunities; abundance; a raise in salary; a spiritual treasure

Reversed: Lack of pleasure from wealth; misspent funds; delays due to a shortage of funds

Two of Coins

Upright: Suggests a choice between alternatives such as careers, job offers, colleges, or relationships; a struggle for balance

Reversed: Juggling obligations; overwhelmed by too many choices; lack of focus

Three of Coins

Upright: Mastery and perfection; a good card for undertaking self-improvement projects and for learning new things, including life lessons

Reversed: Wasteful of time and energy; lack of expertise; slovenliness; carelessness; mediocrity

Four of Coins

Upright: A conservative attitude toward money and risk taking; hoarding and miserliness; may indicate an assessment of self-worth based on material wealth

Reversed: Generosity; largesse; freedom

Five of Coins

Upright: Financial hardship and stress over finances; spiritual wealth in the form of compassion for others less well off

Reversed: Change is on the horizon, bringing opportunities, new ventures, and renewal

Six of Coins

Upright: Meaning varies greatly depending on surrounding cards; change; financial stability; kindness; generosity

Reversed: Ruptured relationship; selfishness; living beyond one's means; lack of saving

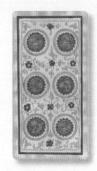

Seven of Coins

Upright: Ingenuity; wise planning; reward for effort; stability; reflection

Reversed: Financial loss; anxiety; instability

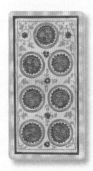

Eight of Coins

Upright: Experienced worker; deep commitment; craftsmanship; apprenticeship and willingness to work and learn; joy from work well done

Reversed: Minimal effort; lack of discipline; usury; intrigue

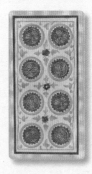

Nine of Coins

Upright: Self-confidence; discretion; safety; comfort; stability

Reversed: Threats and danger; incompletion; miscarriage of pregnancy

Ten of Coins

Upright: Domestic prosperity; success in business

Reversed: Risky venture; bad odds

KNAVE OF COINS

Wearing a large plumed hat, the Knave is shown in profile facing left. He holds a large gold coin at chest height and appears to be examining and admiring its beauty. The pattern on his cloak matches the patterns in the clothing of the other court cards in this suit.

Upright: Scholarly; reflective; practical; capable of deep concentration; a profound curiosity and thirst for knowledge; not afraid to face adversity

Reversed: Immature; lacking in commitment and follow-through; impractical; incapable of sound financial planning

KNIGHT OF COINS

The Knight of Coins is the only court card missing from the original Visconti-Sforza deck. The substitute was re-created by reversing a print of the Knight of Cups and replacing the cups on the cloak with a pattern of Visconti suns interlaced with blue ribbons.

Upright: Good news regarding income; someone mature, responsible, dependable, and organized

Reversed: Lazy; unmotivated; apathetic

QUEEN OF COINS

The Queen sits confidently facing left (the direction of adversity) with a large gold coin resting on her right knee. Her gown is of a similar cloth to that worn by the figures in the other court cards. Woven into the design are blue ribbons winding around the Visconti suns.

Upright: Takes good care of oneself; secure in affluence; content with life; noble; generous. The card also suggests the wisdom of trusting oneself and that applying one's abilities and knowledge will reap the benefits sought.

Reversed: Distrust; lack of self-worth

KING OF COINS

The King of Coins sits facing forward, his legs crossed at the ankles. His short robe is imprinted with the same hexagonal pattern of intertwining deep blue ribbons and Visconti suns as the clothing on the other court cards. The king's left hand rests upon a large gold coin, also imprinted with the Visconti sun.

Upright: An experienced leader; grounded; practical; conservative; might represent a successful professional or businessman having earned substantial material wealth

Reversed: A risk taker who desires money but is unwilling to work for it

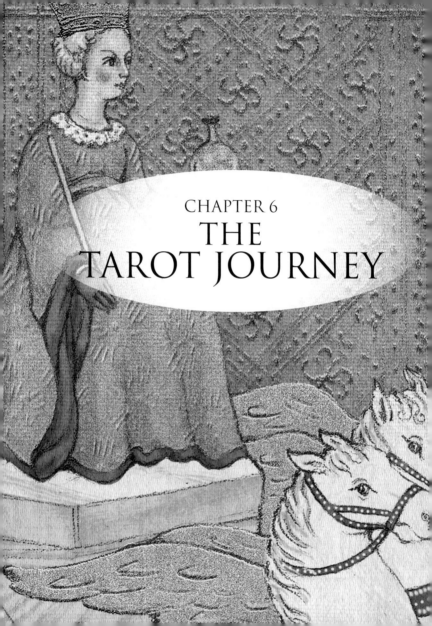

CHAPTER 6
THE
TAROT JOURNEY

"Thoughts without contents are empty, intuitions without concepts are blind. The understanding can intuit nothing, the senses can think nothing. Only through their union can knowledge arise."

— Immanuel Kant

You are about to embark on an inward journey whose destination is your Higher Self. It is this part of you, also known as intuition, that will guide you to your most enlightened decisions. The ultimate goal of reading Tarot is to separate conscious knowledge from the unconscious where your intuition resides. Used wisely, Tarot cards can serve as catalysts to tap into the collective unconscious, or World Soul—that repository of universal knowledge that is a part of us all. Imagine your Tarot cards as portals to your unconscious and Tarot images as their keys.

Opposite page: *A detail from the Chariot card in the Visconti-Sforza deck*

Over the years, the Tarot has sometimes been used for fortune-telling purposes. But since predicting the future is imprecise at best, a better goal of a Tarot reading is to harness your inner wisdom to help make the most of your talents and the choices available to you. A person's reaction to the Tarot is deeply personal, and developing a relationship with the cards takes patience. As the images gradually imprint themselves on your psyche, you will find that you will become more attuned to their significance.

Here are a few helpful hints to speed you on your journey. First, familiarize yourself with the images on the cards and their symbolism. Remember, each trump card is fraught with many layers of meaning. The more time you spend with them, the more their subtleties with be revealed. As you gaze at the cards, you will find that they elicit intuitive reactions. Jot down those feelings as they occur. You might like to have a notebook on hand for just this purpose.

A fun way to acquaint yourself with your cards is to get creative with them. Try linking each trump card with someone you know and jot down the reasons for your choices. Another idea is to divide the court cards and trump figures into two piles: those you'd like to meet at a party and those you'd like to avoid. Again, jot down the reasons. You might also select a card that relates most to your own character or to your particular situation and write about why you were drawn to that card.

Visualization exercises are an excellent way to make use of the cards' power to help with decision making. Perhaps you are feeling overburdened with responsibilities. Make a list of all the places you have to be and all the things you have to do. Before saying yes to another request for your time, find a quiet, peaceful place. Try to block out all mental and visual distractions. Then remove the Hermit card (right) from your deck. Study the card and concentrate on the image of the old man. Now focus on the hourglass. Does it help you find perspective?

There is no single correct way to shuffle Tarot cards. You can shuffle them as you would regular playing cards or, since Tarot cards are larger than playing cards, you might prefer to scatter them facedown on a table and slide them around with your palms until they are well mixed. Do not concern yourself with reverse meanings until you have become a seasoned reader. There are more than enough permutations with the cards in the upright position to allow for a richly meaningful Tarot experience.

Before starting a reading, it is important to be clear about the purpose of your question—the more specific it is, the better. Avoid questions requiring yes or no answers. "What do I need to know about my relationship?" is a better question than "Will my partner and I break up?" "What should I do to improve my chances of getting a promotion?" is better than "Will I get a raise?" "What do I need to understand about my lifestyle?" is better than "Will I lose weight?"

So far, we have been discussing the Tarot as a tool for self-exploration and personal growth. Because this little book is meant to be no more than an introduction to the Tarot, it is best to concentrate on yourself until you are extremely conversant with your cards and their symbolism. The following pages contain several tried-and-true ways to lay out your cards for divination. Remember that all the cards and their sequence in a reading are subject to personal interpretation. There is no right or wrong way to interpret the Tarot. Readings will vary even among professional readers using the same layouts with the same cards. What is important is how the cards resonate with you personally. Your interpretation will depend entirely on your own particular experiences, personality, beliefs, and desires.

THE THREE-CARD SPREAD

The three-card spread is an uncomplicated layout for the beginning Tarot reader. Within this framework, you have the option of choosing in advance what you would like the cards to represent. The questioner shuffles, then deals out three cards, laying them out from left to right. The following list includes several options for focusing a reading:

- Past, present, future
- Situation, attitude, key element
- External conditions, present situation, obstacle
- Body, mind, spirit
- Stop, start, continue
- You, me, us

Here is an elementary example of a three-card reading focusing on the second option: situation, attitude, key element.

Issue: Kevin fears that he will lose his job because several people in his office have been recently laid off. He is stressed because he loves his work and has been putting in extra hours, hoping for a promotion.

His question: What do I need to know about my present work situation?

Card 1, situation: For this card, Kevin turned up the Tower, confirming his assessment that there was upheaval in his workplace.

Card 2, attitude: Here, Kevin turned up the Fool, an indication that he was feeling unsure of himself and was worried about change.

Card 3, key element: The card Kevin turned up here was the Justice card, symbolizing balance and equilibrium. To Kevin, this card meant that he should try to not to let his emotions overtake his judgment.

Outcome: Kevin decided to let go of his fear of change. He would continue working at his current job but would also start networking and sending out his updated resume. By taking positive steps to ensure that he had options, Kevin was able to visualize an optimistic future.

Here is another example of a three-card reading, focusing on the "you, me, us" option.

Issue: Although she has always loved her job, Ellen, a high-school art teacher, has been feeling that she's stuck in a rut.

Her question: What do I need to know about how to relate to my students?

Card 1, you: Ellen turned up the Hanged Man, which she interpreted to mean that her students were in a state of suspended animation, bored with routine, and not engaged with her teaching methods.

Card 2, me: Here, Ellen turned up the Magician, indicating that she should add a bit of excitement to her lesson plans, to try something new to create a bit of "magic" in the classroom.

Card 3, us: For this card, Ellen turned up Temperance, indicating that the relationship between her and her students needed balance.

Outcome: Ellen decided that she would work on becoming more creative in her approach. She would continue to teach technique. Once she was sure that her students understood the basics, however, she would rein in her urge to correct their work and encourage them to bend the rules to free up their creative impulses. The Temperance card inspired Ellen to provide a healthy balance in her classroom in the hope of establishing a happier relationship between her and her students.

1

2   3   4

5

THE FIVE-CARD SPREAD

This is another helpful spread for deciding on a course of action. It works best if the questioner concentrates on one aspect of a decision, choosing from among several possibilities.

Card 1, present/general theme: Deals with the present and states the general theme of the reading

Card 2, past influences: Deals with past forces that are continuing to have an effect

Card 3: the future: Manifests the questioner's future goals

Card 4, reason: Reveals a hidden impulse that may be an obstacle to achieving the questioner's goal

Card 5, potential: Points out the potential outcome if the questioner follows a course of action

SAMPLE READING OF FIVE-CARD SPREAD

Issue: Eric has been dating a woman with whom he thought he was in love. Of late, he has had the feeling that something is not right. The passion has gone out of the relationship, and although he would like to rekindle the spark that once drew them to each other, she seems unwilling to do her part. Eric suspects that she may be interested in someone new.

His question: What do I need to know about my current relationship?

Card 1, present/general theme: The Chariot card turns up in this spot. It fits Eric's present circumstance in that it indicates he is being pulled in two directions. His heart is urging him to stay with the woman he once loved, while his head is telling him that the bond has been broken.

Card 2, past influences: Here, the Eight of Cups indicates that Eric has been aware of trouble in the relationship for some time, and that he is coming to the realization that it has run its course. He is thinking of moving on.

 **Card 3, the future:** In this position, the Four of Batons reveals Eric's desire for a romantic and peaceful relationship with a woman who desires the same.

 **Card 4, reason:** Here, the Six of Cups turns up, suggesting that Eric is clinging to the past, longing for that which is unattainable.

 **Card 5, potential:** In the final position, the Queen of Batons indicates that if Eric lets go of his desire to stay in his present stagnant relationship, a new loving and compassionate woman will come into his life.

Outcome: Eric has decided to give this woman some space. He will spend time pursuing his own interests, renewing old friendships, and making plans that do not involve her. If this cooling-off period spells the end of the relationship, he will accept that fact and move on.

THE CELTIC CROSS

The ten-card spread, also known as the Celtic Cross, dates from the late 1800s. Because it is more complicated than the others, it is best to save this reading until you are comfortable with the simpler ones.

Card 1, the present: Deals with the questioner's present position or provides information about the current conditions in which the questioner lives and works

Card 2, opposing forces: Laid sideways across the first card, it indicates challenges or obstacles

Card 3, goal: Reveals the questioner's subconscious thoughts concerning the reading; laid directly above the questioner, it indicates the questioner's aim for the reading

Card 4, the past: Describes the forces and influences that have helped shape the questioner

Card 5, the recent past: Indicates recent events that may help explain the current situation

Card 6, the future: Reveals a sphere of influence that lies ahead

Card 7, advice: Demonstrates a way to cope with a current fear or worry plaguing the questioner

Card 8, external factors: Indicates how others see the questioner

Card 9, internal factors: Concerns the questioner's emotional states, such as hopes, fears, worries, and possible hidden motives

Card 10, outcome: Weaves together the meanings of the other cards to provide a result; should the outcome be unfavorable, the questioner can change it by applying the wisdom gleaned from the reading

SAMPLE READING OF CELTIC CROSS

Issue: Elizabeth is offered a better paying job in another city, requiring a move.

Her question: What do I need to know to make the right decision for me?

Card 1, the present: The Knight of Batons turns up in this position, fitting Elizabeth's present circumstances in that the card suggests she is poised for a journey into the unknown.

Card 2, opposing forces: Here, the King of Coins represents money and responsibility. In this position, the card tells Elizabeth that in addition to the money she will earn if she accepts the new job, she will have more responsibilities.

Card 3, goal: The Queen of Coins reveals Elizabeth's unconscious desire for luxury and wealth.

Card 4, the past: In this position, the Queen of Cups indicates that in the past, Elizabeth has been a devoted caretaker for her loved ones, putting their well-being before her own wants and needs.

Card 5, the recent past: The Three of Swords suggests that Elizabeth has deferred her dreams by turning down other previously offered jobs that would have advanced her career.

Card 6, the future: Here, the Two of Swords indicates that Elizabeth will achieve greater balance in her life in the future.

Card 7, advice: The Moon reveals that if Elizabeth allows her unconscious feelings to emerge, they will show her how to move forward.

Card 8, external factors: The King of Cups indicates that Elizabeth is seen from the outside as a kind, dependable person.

Card 9, internal factors: In this position, the Ace of Swords reveals Elizabeth's hidden fear of power and success.

Card 10, outcome: The King of Batons is an auspicious card relating to business and enterprise, confirming Elizabeth's leadership and decision-making abilities, leading to the following outcome.

Outcome: If Elizabeth heeds the wisdom revealed in the cards, she will discover truths about herself derived from the reading. She will either decide that she's willing to advance her career by embracing its more stringent demands, confident in her leadership abilities, or she will decide that her unacknowledged and unexpressed desire for wealth is not worth the sacrifice in terms of time and added responsibility. Given that she now has a clearer picture of her innermost desires and her possible choices, whichever decision she makes will provide her with a new-found confidence and maturity.

Acknowledgments

I would like to thank Wald Amberstone of the Tarot School in Manhattan for suggesting that I contact Robert M. Place for help and advice with this project. By far the most knowledgeable and creative of Tarot experts, Robert Place is an internationally known artist, writer, and historian. That he agreed to review my outline and manuscript was beyond gracious. I relied heavily on Robert's books, especially *The Fool's Journey* and *The Tarot: History, Symbolism, and Divination* in my research. I would also like to thank Linda Falken for her help in editing this manuscript. —MP

Further Reading

Alchemy and the Tarot: An Examination of the Historic Connection with a Guide to The Alchemical Tarot by Robert M. Place, Hermes Publications, 2012

The Complete Book of Tarot Reversals by Mary K. Greer, Llewellyn Publications, 2002

The Fool's Journey: The History, Art, & Symbolism of the Tarot by Robert M. Place, Talarius Publications, 2010

Seventy-Eight Degrees of Wisdom: A Book of Tarot by Rachel Pollack, Weiser Books, 2007

The Tarot History, Symbolism, and Divination by Robert M. Place, Tarcher, 2005

The Tarot Revealed: A Beginner's Guide by Paul Fenton-Smith, Allen & Unwin, 2010

Photo Credits